SERVANT
LEADERSHIP
IN THE TWENTY-FIRST CENTURY

Keith Moore

SERVANT
LEADERSHIP
IN THE TWENTY-FIRST CENTURY

Keith Moore

Book layout by Bonnie Bushman
bbushman@bresnan.net

Morgan James Publishing, LLC
1225 Franklin Ave. Ste 325
Garden City, NY 11530-1693
800-485-4943
www.MorganJamesPublishing.com

Habitat
for Humanity®
Peninsula
Building Partner

Moore, Keith.
    Servant Leadership In The Twenty-First
Century/ Keith Moore
    ISBN 1-933596-29-5

TABLE OF CONTENTS

FOREWORD

In this hour the body of Christ is experiencing major shifts in the way we do church, in the way we reach the lost, and in the way we train leaders. Our message has not changed, but thank God our strategies and tactics have. The old structures and paradigms have been torn down and rendered obsolete in this strategic season of harvest. What we are seeing and experiencing is the reestablishment of true biblical order in the Church and in the lives of God's people, as well as the restoration of servant-leadership within the body of Christ.

There is also a critical shifting taking place in the way we equip leadership for the work of the ministry. We see a new and dynamic class of servant-leaders being processed and positioned for global impact in the Twenty-First Century. Gone are the old models of leadership training that focus solely upon the development of "the gift" while failing to develop character. While it is true that your gift will promote you, the fact is that in the Kingdom of God your character alone is what maintains your promotion and ultimately your influence. Today leadership training and character development must be co-joined.

The church is now coming into the knowledge that true leadership is developed through the process of sonship - submitting to authority, enduring chastening and hardships, and for the potential leader to wait patiently for time to intersect with purpose, all resulting in great blessings. Elder Keith Moore is one such leader with great spiritual insight that only comes through the patience and humility of serving others in the Kingdom of God. Jesus has said, "And whosoever of you will be the greatest, shall be servant of all" (Mark 10:44). Elder Moore's book, *Servant Leadership in the Twenty-First Century*, is a testament to his dedication to the servant-leadership model so necessary for Kingdom progression.

The fact is that God is not just interested in raising leaders, but His ultimate goal is to reproduce sons. For it will be the sons who have learned obedience, and the sons who have been loyal, and the sons who have met authority, who are now positioned to lead this next generation of God's people into Destiny Fulfillment.

Embracing People

Expanding Vision

Pursuing Destiny

Bishop Steven W. Banks
Senior Pastor
Living Waters Christian Fellowship
Newport News, Virginia

PASTORAL REFLECTION

I have had the pleasure of watching the Lord build up my spiritual son since leading him to Christ. It is refreshing to hear a word from the Lord from a vessel who is truly a servant within the body of Christ.

For too long the church has been faced with an epidemic of great-minded leaders who are moving in their own self-exaltation. We now have a generation of leaders who are more focused upon themselves than on the Word, the Will, or the Ministry of Jesus. It is a joy to read a book that has been anointed to bring pastors and church leaders back to true biblical greatness.

Jesus said that greatness is contained in the attitude and actions of servant hood. This book will aid you in accepting God's call to you to serve. For those already serving it will provide a much needed wave of refreshing that will renew, revive, and prepare you for the next level of ministry service.

Elder Keith Moore is both an example and ensample of this awesome key to successful ministry. With his most recent book he has provided each of us with the keys we need to unlock the door to corporate ministry, growth, and development.

It is with fatherly pride and godly rejoicing that I highly recommend this wonderful book. Your life and ministry will never be the same as a result of this powerful teaching.

Pastor N. Chris Jordan
Senior Pastor
Unity of Faith Worship Center
Rocky Mount, NC

ACKNOWLEDGMENTS

To say that a book is a labor of love birthed through the efforts of one person is an understatement of epic proportions. This book is no different. If it had not been for those men and women who sowed into my life and this vision with their time, talents, and gifts this book would not have been possible.

Above all else, I give praise, honor, and glory unto He who is, was, and is yet to come! There is no higher calling than to do the will of the Father, and I am so very thankful for this opportunity to yet again pen His words and share His heart with you. I pray this work edifies you and glorifies God. I thank God for giving me a voice and for blessing me to lead by example and serve according to His good pleasure.

To my wife Connie, you are my inspiration. In the midnights of my life you have been there encouraging, embracing, and fortifying me for the journey ahead. Your unconditional love and acceptance of all that I am as a man, a husband, and a minister of the gospel have propelled me to greatness. To my children, Keith Jr. and Keilah, you are my joy, my inheritance, my true riches.

To my pastors, Bishop Steven W. Banks and Pastor Keira Taylor-Banks, I thank you for entrusting me with the heart of this ministry. I will always remain your faithful servant. To Pastor Chris Jordan, you knew me before I really knew myself. You encouraged and provoked me to put God first and allow Him to direct my paths.

To my mother, I take a piece of you everywhere I go; your words of strength resonate within me.

I am grateful to Adria Strothers, my editor, who ensures that the order is right. Beverly T. Gooden, Reganda Smith and Margie Jones - the knights of the round table- have my undying gratitude for their editing and input. To Stephen Blackmon, our webmaster and graphics specialist, you are awesome. For my spiritual big sister in Christ, Sharrin Owens, your technical and video expertise is invaluable. To Elder Mark Troublefield, the one who taught me everything that I know, I am grateful for your example of servant hood and many words of wisdom over the years and in this project. And to the wordsmith, Mary DeAllfordii, I just say thank you for making yourself available and allowing God to use you tremendously. You have been a valuable asset from day one, and I am excited about your project!

Lastly, I give thanks for every reader of this book. If I am able to make any impact, no matter how small, then every sacrifice, every tear, and every hurt was worth it.

INTRODUCTION

In the Old Testament an armourbearer was an officer selected by kings and generals because of his bravery. His purpose was to bear the armour and stand by his leader in the time of danger. An armourbearer was in charge of sharpening and carrying his leader's weapons. He was an extension of help because he provided more *arms*. As illustrated in the Old Testament, the armourbearer was more involved in the physical aspect of fighting than the spiritual.

In contrast, modern day armourbearers are called to function more on the spiritual aspect than the physical. They are called to assist in carrying the load of their leaders. Armourbearers are also known as adjutants, pastor's personal aides-ppa- and helps ministry in the body of Christ.

In looking at Jesus' ministry, we observe the inner court, the outer court, and the multitudes. I see an analogy between Jesus' interactions with the people and a pastor's interaction with his congregation. Peter, James, and John – the inner court – had direct access to the private chambers with Jesus. The remaining nine disciples made up the outer court, and the multitude consisted of the other followers of Jesus. Likewise, these three extensions are found in today's ministries.

Because armourbearers have direct access to their leader's private chambers they make up the inner court. The leadership within a congregation generally makes up the outer court. They have access to their leader but may not be exposed to his private chambers. Lastly, the congregation consists of the multitude because even though they are a part of the assembly they may not have total access to their leader.

Over the last several years I have had the honor of serving as my pastor's armourbearer. Through my personal experiences and research I have discovered that the purpose of an armourbearer is to release and free the man of God by providing practical ministry designed to meet his spiritual, physical, and personal needs. In this book I will highlight the attributes and the ministry of an armourbearer. Even though this book is written from the perspective of an armourbearer, every believer has a part to play in serving his leader (Ephesians 4:16).

CHAPTER 1
HEART OF AN ARMOURBEARER

And his armourbearer said unto him, Do
all that is in thine heart: turn thee; behold,
I am with thee according to thy heart.
1 Samuel 14:7

Entering into salvation is the first step in a person's life. The next step is to get connected to a local body of Christ and begin serving in a ministry. As you become more connected to your church, you take on the spirit of your leader. This is important because it is difficult for an armourbearer to serve his leader without having his heart. As stated in Amos 3:3, *"Can two walk together, except they be agreed?"* The heart of an armourbearer is illustrated in 1 Samuel 14:7 when Jonathan's armourbearer stated that he was with him with all his heart.

It is dangerous to be close to your leader and not have a heart connection. Envy, selfishness, discord, and jealousy can enter your heart if you do not have your leader's heart. For example, Judas Iscariot lost his heart connection with Jesus and experienced a violent death. The Bible advises us to *keep our heart with all diligence, for out of it are the issues of life* (Proverbs 4:23). In contrast to Judas, the disciple John remained connected to Jesus and loved him so much that he was called the beloved disciple and had the privilege to lay his head on Jesus' bosom.

1

CHAPTER LIFE APPLICATIONS

_____

_____

_____

_____

_____

_____

_____

_____

_____

_____

_____

_____

_____

_____

_____

CHAPTER 2
CALL OF AN ARMOURBEARER

And David came to Saul, and stood before him: and he loved him greatly; and he became his armourbearer.
1 Samuel 16:21

After the heart of a believer is revealed to his leader, the decision may be made to appoint him as an armourbearer. We see an example of this in 1 Samuel 16:21. From this passage we see that David was appointed as Saul's armourbearer because he loved Saul and was connected to him.

In general, we know that any leadership position requires a call from God. Let us look at Numbers 11:16-17 which states:

And the LORD said unto Moses, Gather unto me seventy men of the elders of Israel, whom thou knowest to be the elders of the people, and officers over them; and bring them unto the tabernacle of the congregation, that they may stand there with thee. And I will come down and talk with thee there: and I will take of the spirit which is upon thee, and will put it upon them; and they shall bear the burden of the people with thee, that thou bear it not thyself alone.

In this passage the leaders who had a heart connection to Moses were appointed to assist him in his ministry. Furthermore, in the New Testament Jesus called the disciples

3

who walked beside Him and assisted Him with His needs just as an armourbearer assists his leader (Matthew 4:18-19).

An example of this was on the day Jesus called Peter while he was out fishing. Peter made a conscious decision to follow Jesus when He told him to drop his nets. Peter could have remained a fisherman, but he chose to become a fisher of men.

It is essential in our contemporary church to recognize that every joint supplies (Ephesians 4:16). At its core every member has been called to minister. The word minister means to wait upon. Just as Jesus called Peter to minister, He is still calling each of us to serve as waiters within the body of Christ. Whether you are an armourbearer, an usher, a children's worker, or a deacon you have a respective calling and must make a conscious decision whether you will accept and heed the call.

Lastly, we all must acknowledge that just as we have differing gifts, abilities, and talents our calling is uniquely our own. There should not be any contentiousness, jealousy, or discord within the church because every minister must work in conjunction with others to further the Kingdom (1 Corinthians 12:12-20). Likewise, our natural body has many parts that all work in conjunction to fulfill its purpose.

CHAPTER LIFE APPLICATIONS

_____

_____

_____

_____

_____

_____

_____

_____

_____

_____

_____

_____

_____

_____

_____

_____

_____

CHAPTER 3
COMMITMENT OF AN ARMOURBEARER

O Timothy, keep that which is committed to thy trust, avoiding profane and vain babblings, and oppositions of science falsely so called:
1 Timothy 6:20

Once you have accepted the clarion call for your life it is important to clearly understand the requirement and the commitment level that is expected of you. In Hebrew, commitment means a duty to serve another person even when times are not convenient to do so.

Commitment fosters love because you will never be committed to someone you do not love. Taking a look at John's love for Jesus, we see that his love brought him into a true commitment to the degree that John's whole life consisted of pointing people to Jesus. John personified agape love. It was this type of love in its purest form that set John apart even from the other disciples.

True commitment is birthed through testing and trials and prefers other people before itself (1 Kings 17:7-13). When Jesus was in the Garden of Gethsemane He submitted Himself to the will of the Father out of a pure love for each of us even though He knew what was about to befall Him.

I know from experience that what you do for your leader God will do for you. Because of my service to my pastor I was blessed with divine favor in the writing and release of my first book. While serving my pastor I was granted access to many anointed vessels of God. God used these same people to assist me in furthering the gospel in the ministry that He was birthing in me.

Trust is the foundation of all commitment. Regardless of your role in the ministry you must establish trust in your leader. After trust has been established, you must develop faith in your leader. Faith is a by-product of proving your relationship. From faith comes true allegiance which says, ***"Yet though he slay me, I will trust Him"*** (Job 13:15).

Being committed to your leader is similar to commitment in a marriage. For example, in a marriage a man and woman are yoked together. Likewise, you must be yoked to your leader. Furthermore, even though you spoke words of commitment at the altar it is not until that commitment is tested that it is cemented and made whole.

With highly visible ministries like that of the armourbearer you only see one side and are not exposed to what goes on outside of the church. It is not until you begin serving that the true cost of service is revealed. For many it is the hard work that separates the truly committed from those seeking a position. Frequently an individual may not be able to maintain his level of commitment because his flesh is undisciplined. True commitment does not allow anything to deter it.

CHAPTER LIFE APPLICATIONS

_____

_____

_____

_____

_____

_____

_____

_____

_____

_____

_____

_____

_____

_____

_____

_____

CHAPTER 4
ATTRIBUTES OF AN ARMOURBEARER

Trustworthiness

*And Ham, the father of Canaan, saw the nakedness of
his father, and told his two brethren without.
And Shem and Japheth took a garment, and laid it upon
both their shoulders, and went backward, and covered
the nakedness of their father; and their faces were
backward, and they saw not their father's nakedness.*
Genesis 9:22-23

As an armourbearer you must be able to hold the
confidence of your leader and others and operate out of a
spirit of confidentiality. You may hear things that you will
never be able to repeat. Your leader must know that he can
be himself around you and trust you totally. For example,
your leader may have private conversations with others
while you are in the car with him, or he may minister to
people at the altar. Because you are in close proximity to
him you must never share these private conversations with
others. It has been said that there are some things that you
must take to your grave with you.

Because you may be privy to the affairs of others you
must not allow this information to change your feelings

about that person or become judgmental of them. But you must continue loving and praying for them.

You may also see your leader's vulnerabilities, his highs and lows, his ups and downs. He may be spiritually exposed before you just as Noah was exposed, but you must understand that you are there to provide a level of covering as illustrated by Shem and Japheth in Genesis 9:20-24.

As a result of the release of the Holy Spirit your leader may be drained and in need of physical and spiritual replenishment after ministering. An armourbearer must remain spiritually vigilant over his leader during this time. He must comprehend that his leader may be highly susceptible to other forces because of the demand that has been made upon him. You must be ready to minister to him and his needs.

CHAPTER LIFE APPLICATIONS

_____

_____

_____

_____

_____

_____

_____

_____

_____

_____

_____

_____

_____

_____

_____

CHAPTER 5
ATTRIBUTES OF AN ARMOURBEARER

Faithfulness

***Moreover it is required in stewards, that a
man be found faithful.***
1 Corinthians 4:2

Because there will be numerous times when your leader will call upon you an armourbearer must be faithful. Your leader needs to be assured that he can depend upon you for even the most innocuous tasks. He should be able to rest easy and trust in you to achieve the desired results.

As found in Genesis 24:3-5, Abraham entrusted his servant to find a wife for Isaac, his son. One of the most important and life-changing events anyone will ever undergo was placed in the hands of his servant. Why did Abraham do this? He did it because he knew that his servant was in tune with his heart and would know what was acceptable.

Therefore, we see that faithfulness is a condition of the heart. The fruit of the heart is evidenced by your willingness to submit and cast aside your own personal goals and objectives for the good of another. A faithful armourbearer is one who denies himself for the greater vision of his leader. Looking at the relationship between Timothy and Paul, we see that Timothy served as Paul's armourbearer. He demonstrated his connection to Paul through his faithfulness and it was this that propelled him as one of the greatest young ministers in the early church. His greatness rested in his ability to follow. He was wholly sold out to the vision.

Faithfulness is a prerequisite for elevation. As a result of his faithfulness, God blessed Timothy with his own ministry (Philippians 2:19-23). The launching of Timothy into his own ministry is pinpointed in 1 Thessalonians 3:1-2. The Bible lets us know that, *"He who is faithful in a very little [thing] is faithful also in much, and he who is dishonest and unjust in a very little [thing] is dishonest and unjust also in much. Therefore if you have not been faithful in the [case of] unrighteous mammon (deceitful riches, money, possessions), who will entrust to you the true riches?"* (Luke 16:10-12 Amplified Bible)

Joshua is another example of the importance of faithfulness in service. The Bible refers to him as Moses' minister and in this capacity he carried out Moses' instructions to the letter. There is no evidence to suggest that Joshua ever acted under his own stead but rather at the command of Moses.

Whether Joshua was in the valley fighting against the enemies of the Lord, spying out the land, or leading the people Moses trusted Joshua. Joshua echoed the voice of Moses (Exodus 17:10) before the people and it was his willingness to submit himself to Moses' authority that catapulted him to greater glory in the end as he led the people into the Promised Land.

CHAPTER LIFE APPLICATIONS

_____

_____

_____

_____

_____

_____

_____

_____

_____

_____

_____

_____

_____

_____

_____

CHAPTER 6
ATTRIBUTES OF AN ARMOURBEARER

Persistence

And the three mighty men brake through the host of the Philistines, and drew water out of the well of Bethlehem, that was by the gate, and took it, and brought it to David: nevertheless he would not drink thereof, but poured it out unto the LORD.
1 Samuel 23:16

A true armourbearer never uses the word *why*. Isaiah 6:8 should be indelibly etched upon the hearts and minds of every armourbearer. When given a task an armourbearer doesn't ask how or why; he makes it happen. The difficulty of the assignment is never an issue; you must be ready to move in an effort to achieve success.

My definition of persistence is to make something happen no matter what it takes. Joshua possessed this spirit. Moses spoke it; Joshua did it and brought it to pass. There is no written evidence that he once questioned Moses as to why or how? He depended upon the Holy Spirit to empower him to bring it to pass.

The entire sixth chapter of the book of Joshua is a living testimony to the power of a make-it-happen attitude within

19

the body of Christ. Joshua spoke, the people did, and a great victory was wrought for the glory of God. There was no dissent in the ranks; no one was espousing their own philosophies. There were no new ideas, counterproductive debates, or referendums.

David's mighty men of valor provide further tangible proof of a make-it-happen spirit as found in 2 Samuel 23:14:

"And David was then in an hold, and the garrison of the Philistines was then in Bethlehem. And David longed, and said, Oh that one would give me drink of the water of the well of Bethlehem, which is by the gate! And the three mighty men brake through the host of the Philistines, and drew water out of the well of Bethlehem, that was by the gate, and took it, and brought it to David: nevertheless he would not drink thereof, but poured it out unto the LORD. And he said, Be it far from me, O LORD, that I should do this: is not this the blood of the men that went in jeopardy of their lives? therefore he would not drink it."

When you accept the call to serve in any capacity within the body of Christ you must be willing to go the distance for your ministry. Whatever is necessary to bring about the desired results is your responsibility to do it and to provide it. You do not have a right to sit back complacently and complain about what is lacking or hindering you from moving forward. Rather you must be willing to overcome obstacles, circumvent pitfalls, climb higher heights, and go to deeper depths to make it happen. We must practice Nike's slogan, "Just do it!"

CHAPTER LIFE APPLICATIONS

_____

_____

_____

_____

_____

_____

_____

_____

_____

_____

_____

_____

_____

_____

_____

_____

CHAPTER 7
PRAY FOR YOUR LEADER

I exhort therefore, that, first of all, supplications,
prayers, intercessions, and giving of thanks,
be made for all men;
For kings, and for all that are in authority;
that we may lead a quiet and peaceable life
in all godliness and honesty.
1 Timothy 2:1-2

Within the body of Christ there is a call of the Father to pray. Prayer is not limited to a select group within the body but is a commandment for all. God requires that you develop a personal prayer life through which He speaks, directs, admonishes, corrects, and empowers. Prayer is perpetual according to 1 Thessalonians 5:17. If we consider prayer as a time of intimacy and sharing with the Father we recognize that without it there can be no power to overcome the enemy's devices.

As an armourbearer you must flex and strengthen your intercessory prayer muscles and stand in the gap for your leader. This is not a hit or miss thing but requires that you have the same level of discipline a bodybuilder exhibits when he is in training.

Traditionally speaking, the armourbearer carried the physical armaments of the one he was protecting. This ancient day armourbearer recognized that his leader was a warrior. Likewise, because your leader is a warrior in a battle he needs an armourbearer too. In the past as well as today, many in the body of Christ overlook the importance of the ministry of an armourbearer because they fail to understand this very concept.

Ephesians 6:12-17 illustrates the level of combat we endure. We must be fully girded in the whole armor of God, and we are not properly equipped if we are not seeking out a divine connection through daily prayer.

No one should ever doubt or deny the power of prayer or lack thereof. You have a responsibility to intercede for your leader's protection, peace, power, revelation, and ongoing connection with the Holy Spirit. Ask the Holy Spirit to guide your leader in his day-to-day activities.

When Jesus came to Gethsemane right before He made preparations to go to the cross He asked his disciples to pray for him. There will be times when much prayer is needed for your leader when things are going on in the ministry.

Prayer is so important because it dispatches angels on your behalf to cover the man of God. Without prayer the man of God is open to attacks from the devil. As armourbearers and believers in the body of Christ we are all called to pray for our leader because his assignment is much greater than ours, and he has more responsibility than we do.

Let's look at some people of prayer in the Bible. In Acts 12:5 the saints made intercession for Peter and as a result he was released from prison. Likewise, Paul understood the power of prayer and continuously sought out the prayers of the saints (Romans 15:30) and stood in the gap for them.

You must cover your leader in prayer just as Paul prayed for others. Imagine the outcome of your ongoing prayers (James 5:16). More souls would be saved, bodies healed, and marriages restored through much prayer. Just as Paul depended upon prayer to lead the first century church, we need it more than ever in these last and evil days as we are fighting twenty-first century devils.

I will point out some nuggets that you should pray for your leader.

- Pray that intercession and giving of thanks be made for your leader (1 Timothy 2:1).

- Pray that he leads a quiet and peaceable life in all godliness and honesty (1 Timothy 2:2).

- Pray that the word of the Lord may have free course in his life and be glorified in the earth through him (2 Thessalonians 3:1).

- Pray that he is delivered from unreasonable and wicked men (2 Thessalonians 3:2).

- Pray that he can open his mouth boldly to make known the gospel to the world (Ephesians 6:20, Acts19:8).

- Pray that his faith will increase to fulfill his God given vision (Luke 17:5).

CHAPTER LIFE APPLICATIONS

_____

_____

_____

_____

_____

_____

_____

_____

_____

_____

_____

_____

_____

_____

CHAPTER 8
STUDY YOUR LEADER

Those things, which ye have both learned, and received, and heard, and seen in me, do: and the God of peace shall be with you.
Philippians 4:9

An armourbearer must take the time to study his leader. He must know what his leader wants before he asks for it and understand his posture and ways. He must know when to talk and when not to talk. I have learned from experience to let my leader lead in conversation and to follow his lead if he wants to talk.

An armourbearer should know his leader better than anyone else knows him because he spends more time with him than anyone else except his family. It is helpful to know what things he needs for ministering and what he likes personally. Then you will be ahead of the game when he asks you to get something for him.

It really frustrates me when my leader asks me something and I do not know the answer, or he asks for something and I do not have it. That is why it is imperative that you take the time to learn the needs of your leader such as: his itinerary, the foods and drinks that he likes, the restaurants he likes to visit, and so on. It may also be helpful to keep the phone numbers' of these restaurants, car washes, and dry cleaners in your cell phone or at your disposal.

I like to have a copy of my leader's daily, short-range, and long-range itinerary. This frees him up from thinking about his daily activities if he knows that I know it. It also affords me the opportunity to make sure that someone will be available to assist him and to travel with him.

It is also important to know how your leader flows and what frustrates him. You must maintain eye contact with him so that you can learn to communicate with him through his eyes and body language. By doing this you will enter in sync with him so that you can recognize his need without him speaking it. Eye contact and body language are also important in recognizing the things that may frustrate your leader. By studying your leader you will free him up spiritually, physically, and mentally and prevent distractions while he is ministering.

CHAPTER LIFE APPLICATIONS

_____

_____

_____

_____

_____

_____

_____

_____

_____

_____

_____

_____

_____

_____

_____

_____

_____

CHAPTER 9
PROTECT YOUR LEADER

But Abishai the son of Zeruiah succoured him, and smote the Philistine, and killed him. Then the men of David sware unto him, saying, Thou shalt go no more out with us to battle, that thou quench not the light of Israel.
2 Samuel 21:17

In this chapter we will address some practical measures of protecting your leader. First, let us look at how you can provide coverage while you are in the presence of your leader. When you are walking with your leader you should always walk behind him because it is easier to see him from every angle. If something happens you can easily step in front of him and cut someone off rather than trying to step behind him. A natural example is when we see the president walking; the secret service is always walking behind him. Another reason why we walk behind our leader is because it is a place of humility and submission. Armourbearers should also keep a proper angle for total coverage. Always know where the exits are and know how to get to the quickest one.

While in church you cannot get caught up in the order of service. Your attention must be on your leader which means that your eyes must remain open at all times. How do you expect to protect someone when you cannot see him? Do you think that the president's bodyguards can close their eyes or take their eyes off of him? The answer is no because someone is always waiting to catch them off guard. Likewise, the enemy is watching you to catch you unaware.

Another way to protect your leader is to take care of situations that may arise so that he does not have to deal with them. For example, an irate person may have entered the building before service and asked to speak to the pastor. You can redirect this person to someone else so that your pastor will not have to deal with this before he ministers. Another example may be if someone speaks harsh words about your leader. You are there to let them know that they are not to speak against the Lord's anointed (Numbers 12:1-2). Miriam was cursed with leprosy because she spoke against her leader.

CHAPTER LIFE APPLICATIONS

_____

_____

_____

_____

_____

_____

_____

_____

_____

_____

_____

_____

_____

_____

_____

CHAPTER 10
SUPPORT YOUR LEADER

So Joshua did as Moses had said to him, and fought with Amalek: and Moses, Aaron, and Hur went up to the top of the hill. And it came to pass, when Moses held up his hand, that Israel prevailed: and when he let down his hand, Amalek prevailed.
Exodus 17:10-11

In this chapter we will look at some ways that you can support your leader physically. Your leader needs your physical, spiritual, and financial support. He needs to know that he can depend on you at all times.

In the scripture above we see an example of physical support for your leader. While in a battle with their enemy Aaron and Hur learned how to support their leader. When Moses' hands went down the Amalekites prevailed, but when his hands were up the Israelites prevailed. It was at this time that Aaron and Hur perceived what was happening and supported Moses by keeping his hands uplifted. Aaron and Hur could have taken this opportunity to try to replace Moses, but they did not. They remained in their lane and supported the man of God.

Moses became physically weak during this battle, and as a result it affected him spiritually. When Moses, the leader, became weak the people were defeated. Likewise, if your leader becomes weak the congregation can become defeated or open to attack. We can also relate this to a flock that is open to attack if the shepherd becomes weak. On the other hand, if your leader is strong most likely the congregation will be strong.

Another revelation that I received from this passage is that not everyone can go to the top of the mountain with his leader. Moses chose Aaron and Hur to go with him because he knew they could deal with witnessing the vulnerability of their leader. In the New Testament Jesus took Peter, James, and John to the mountain where he was transfigured before them because they were the only ones that could handle the **weighty** things of God.

Some other ways that you can support your leader physically may include: driving him to and from engagements, taking care of his cars by washing them or putting gas in them, helping him with the yard work, picking up his clothes from the dry cleaners, and anything else that needs to be done to free up his time. I know some people are going to say, "He can cut his own grass or wash his own car." Do you think the president washes his car or cuts his grass? How much more important is my man of God to me than the president? There is no way that you can count the cost for the many lives that have been transformed by the ministry of your leader (1 Timothy 5:17). Just look at what the man of God has done for you and your family and friends. I know first hand how blessed I am because of my leader and the way I serve him.

I am not making light of the job of president or other people who require personal assistants. I am just saying that it is time for the body of Christ to realize that our leaders are gifts from God and that we need to take care of them (Ephesians 4:8-11). Because everyone has unique needs, you can discover the needs of your leader by communicating with him.

Another way that you can support your leader is through financial means. Matthew 6:21 says where your treasures are your heart will be also. By sowing into your leader you are demonstrating that you treasure his ministry and that he is worthy of the rewards that go along with giving up everything to follow the Lord (1 Timothy 5:18).

CHAPTER LIFE APPLICATIONS

_____

_____

_____

_____

_____

_____

_____

_____

_____

_____

_____

_____

_____

_____

_____

_____

CHAPTER 11
SACRIFICE FOR YOUR LEADER

Then said Jesus unto his disciples, If any man will come after me, let him deny himself, and take up his cross, and follow me. For whosoever will save his life shall lose it: and whosoever will lose his life for my sake shall find it.
Matthew 16:24

In the previous chapter we discussed supporting your leader, and in this chapter we will discuss sacrifices. When we talk about sacrifices we can learn from our Lord and Savior Jesus Christ, the greatest example, who sacrificed His life for us.

Matthew 16:24 demonstrates that sacrifice involves denying yourself for a greater cause. John the Baptist illustrated this concept when he gave up his entire life to pave the way for Jesus. John was called the greatest born of women. Why? It was because his whole purpose was to release Jesus into his messianic call.

There are many of us who desire to be great in the kingdom like Jesus and John the Baptist. How is this greatness attained? We find the answer in Matthew 20:26 which states, *But it shall not be so among you: but whosoever will be great among you, let him be your minister.* So we see that the greatest in the kingdom is a servant.

I have had to grasp this concept as well. There have been times when my man of God called; my body was tired and I did not want to go. I learned that a sacrifice is not a sacrifice unless it costs. Remember that because Jesus understood sacrifice it cost Him His life. Most of us may not be asked to go this far, but God wants us to be **willing** to lose our life for His sake.

An armourbearer must be willing to sacrifice himself, his time, and his talents; he must learn to put the kingdom things first. The Bible says in Matthew 6:33 to *seek first the kingdom of God {His way of doing things} and his righteousness; and all these things shall be added unto you* (Amplified Bible). Many people make themselves available with their mouths, however, when it is time to work they always seem to make excuses.

David understood sacrifice when he courageously fought Goliath. David's men also understood sacrifice when they put their lives on the line for him in battle (2 Samuel 21:17).

CHAPTER LIFE APPLICATIONS

_____

_____

_____

_____

_____

_____

_____

_____

_____

_____

_____

_____

_____

_____

CHAPTER 12
SUBMIT TO YOUR LEADER

Obey them that have the rule over you, and submit yourselves: for they watch for your souls, as they that must give account, that they may do it with joy, and not with grief: for that is unprofitable for you.
Hebrews 13:17

The scripture above tells us to submit to our leader. Submission is profitable for us and brings joy to our leader.

In the Bible we see several examples of servants who submitted to their leaders. Joshua submitted to Moses (Exodus 17:10). As a result, he became the successor of Israel (Joshua 1:1-2). David submitted to Saul as his armourbearer. Even though David had already been anointed as king he had to first submit to the delegated authority before he could walk in the anointing as king. God used David's armourbearer ministry to prepare him for his position as king (1 Sam 16:11-21).

Timothy's effectiveness and greatness in the kingdom came as a result of his submission to Paul. I believe that it was not Timothy's desire at first to become a minister through his serving Paul. It was Paul who saw the calling on Timothy's life. Because Timothy served Paul, Paul was released to write many letters or epistles. It also released Timothy to his ministry.

I have noticed over the years that as I submitted to my leader that God started birthing something in my life. I learned that the ministry that God had placed on the inside of me was like a seed that was buried underground in the soil. In John 12:24 it says *"...except a corn of wheat fall into the ground and die, it abideth alone: but if it die, it bringeth forth much fruit."* My interpretation of this scripture is that unless you bury your vision into another man's vision you will never produce fruit.

It has been said that submission means "coming under another person's mission". A person with a prideful or jealous spirit will find it difficult to submit to another man. King Saul was an example of someone who struggled with total submission.

In other words, even though you may have a vision you must first submit to the greater vision. As I submitted to the higher vision of my leader I began to see my personal ministry come to pass.

CHAPTER LIFE APPLICATIONS

_____

_____

_____

_____

_____

_____

_____

_____

_____

_____

_____

_____

_____

_____

_____

CHAPTER 13

BLESSINGS OF AN ARMOURBEARER

...Believe in the LORD your God, so shall ye be established; believe his prophets, so shall ye prosper.
2 Chronicles 20:20b

Your blessings are connected to the leader you serve, and your blessings can only be received based on your perception of your leader. When we talk about blessings most people automatically think about money. But I will establish that blessings can also manifest themselves through favor, healing, or miracles.

The Bible says in 2 Chronicles 20:20, *"...believe in the LORD your God, so shall ye be established; believe his prophets, so shall ye prosper."* The widow of Zarephath believed the word of the Lord from the prophet Elijah when she was asked to borrow many vessels that would later be filled with oil. As a result, the widow had enough oil to use to pay her debt and live off the rest (2 Kings 4:1-7). I have personally seen the blessings and favor on my life because I accepted the call to serve my leader.

In 2 Kings 2:9-10 Elisha received a double portion of Elijah's spirit because of his connection to Elijah. This promise was conditional because in order for Elisha to receive this he had to see Elijah when he was taken away.

The phrase 'if you see me' deals with Elisha's availability.

Matthew 8:8 establishes that blessings are a result of servant hood. The centurion's servant became ill. Due to the connection he had with his servant, the centurion interceded by going to Jesus and proclaiming, *"...but speak the word only and my servant shall be healed."* As a result, the servant was healed.

Even though your blessings are based on your connection in order to receive them you must perceive that your leader is a man of God. Matthew 10:41 states, *"He that receiveth a prophet in the name of a prophet shall receive a prophet's reward; and he that receiveth a righteous man in the name of a righteous man shall receive a righteous man's reward."* Because the Shunammite woman perceived Elisha as a man of God she prepared a chamber for him. As a result of her perception of Elisha, the Shunammite woman was blessed with a son. One day this woman's son died unexpectedly and because the woman had taken care of Elisha God used Elisha to perform a miracle and bring her son back to life (2 Kings 4:18-37).

CHAPTER LIFE APPLICATIONS

_____

_____

_____

_____

_____

_____

_____

_____

_____

_____

_____

_____

_____

_____

_____

_____

CHAPTER 14
PRESENCE OF AN ARMOURBEARER

And Jonathan climbed up upon his hands and upon his feet, and his armourbearer after him: and they fell before Jonathan; and his armourbearer slew after him.
1 Samuel 14:13

More than any other individual role the armourbearer must be seen and not heard, speaking only when given the liberty by his man of God. I am not saying you have to be a robot or puppet, but your role is to guard the man of God both spiritually and physically. As an armourbearer your personal thoughts are not part of the ministry. Although there will be private times when your leader may call upon you to speak into his life, your ministry is not one of being a conversationalist. If you are always spending time offering your opinion when one is not asked for then how will you be able to totally focus on your primary role of serving your man of God?

There will be times when it is appropriate for you to speak; this is not the time for personal thoughts. An armour-bearer must practice wisdom in speech as well as in his character when it comes to speaking. Before uttering a word remember Proverbs 15:2 which states that, *"The tongue of the wise uses knowledge rightly, but the mouth of fools pours forth foolishness" (Spirit Filled Life Bible, New King James Version).*

An armourbearer must remember that he is there to serve and observe his surroundings by listening and responding to situations rather than reacting to them. To respond is to be ready for a situation or anticipate it. Whereas, reacting to a situation is to be caught by surprise or unaware. You want to always respond rather than react. You can always act faster when you are prepared to respond to a situation rather than react to it. This can only be accomplished by being sensitive to the leading of the Holy Spirit through prayer and through knowing your leader. The goal here is to stay one or two steps ahead of what is actually happening.

There will be occasions when you will have to use your mouth in order to deal with particular situations. It is at these times when you need to step up to the plate and use your God-given gift to ward off such intrusions.

Church members need to understand that bringing their concerns or problems to the man of God immediately before and/or after he has ministered is bad timing. Although most church members are aware of proper protocol, there will be times when you must verbally assert yourself to others to ensure they are aware of it. At these times you do not need anyone to tell you it is okay to take the proper action. Be seen but not heard!

You must practice and master the ability to speak discreetly and not become noticeable of doing your job. You must verbally direct others away from your leader when it is appropriate to do so with love so that you do not appear to be disrespectful. When you are able to remove a distraction or potentially embarrassing act in love and with the right spirit you will be more respected and your ministry to others will be better understood.

Once you gain the experience of truly knowing your leader the Lord will impart into your spirit His wisdom to know when and where it is appropriate to speak. For example, years ago while serving as my pastor's armourbearer the Lord instilled in me a sense of knowing when and where it is appropriate to speak. I thought it was my own instinct but later learned that the Lord was teaching me proper conduct and behavior whenever I was with my pastor. There were times when I would drive from place to place for several hours with my pastor and there was very little conversation. I could not take it personal and think that he did not want to talk to me, but I learned to respect his quiet time of reflection and meditation. Even in the presence of other pastors who had gotten to know me over the years I had to be careful not to conduct myself inappropriately in speech or behavior.

There would also be times when it was just the two of us and my pastor would ask for my feelings about things that were taking place in our church, or he would just want to know how I was doing personally. It was at these times when he gave me the liberty to speak freely and not just "tell him what he wanted to hear." These were times that I treasure to this day because they were also times where he spoke into my life personally to encourage me. An armourbearer needs to treasure these private times because it is at these times when your man of God will impart personally into your life and share his own private thoughts.

When you are able to master the ability to be seen and not heard and display the appropriate behavior and conduct expected of an armourbearer, God will begin to honor your service and life in ways you cannot imagine. Always remember that anyone can open his mouth to speak, but few are able to keep it closed when it is appropriate to do so. A true armourbearer should stand out in a crowd not because of what he says but because of what he does not say.

CHAPTER LIFE APPLICATIONS

_____

_____

_____

_____

_____

_____

_____

_____

_____

_____

_____

_____

_____

_____

_____

CHAPTER 15
WIFE OF AN ARMOURBEARER

Can two walk together, except they be agreed?
Amos 3:3

Note: This chapter was written with the assistance of my wife so that you could see the important role that an armourbearer's wife plays.

When I was first asked to serve as one of my pastor's armourbearers I had no idea what to expect and neither did my wife. Neither one of us had been exposed to the armourbearer's ministry; therefore, we had no point of reference. We had to rely on the Holy Spirit to teach us. The closest reference point that my wife had was the example of submission that was demonstrated by our first lady.

It was through our first lady's example that my wife learned to release me to do what God had called me to do. She understood that if she did not release me she would frustrate the call of God on my life and would prevent me from freely assisting the man of God the way that I needed to do. She had observed the way that our first lady released our pastor, so she followed her example and released me.

My wife asked herself, "Why does the congregation expect the first lady to share her husband, but yet no one else wants to share their husbands?" She received the revelation that everyone has a part to contribute in the kingdom and that every joint supplies, therefore, she freely released me to do the work of my ministry. Keep in mind that the pastor equips us to do the work of the ministry. Therefore, no matter what role your spouse has been assigned to do in the kingdom release him so that the kingdom of God can be advanced.

My wife and I have seen many armourbearers come and go. Some left because their season was up, some left because they missed God, or others left because they had spouses who did not want to release their husbands. Because of this my wife and I now choose to converse with newly appointed armourbearers and their wives. We want to make sure that both of them understand what is expected and that they are in agreement with the expectations.

We also experience others who try to get close to me so that they too can be appointed as an armourbearer. We know that they are only looking at the outward appearance and have no clue what it really takes to serve a man of God who is going somewhere. We tell them not to covet what others have because they don't know what they went through to get it. We also tell them that not everyone is called to be an armourbearer. Therefore, rather than desiring to do what someone else is doing they need to seek God's face for what He has for them. Anytime you try to do what you are not called to do it is going to be a struggle.

My wife was in agreement with me when I accepted the call to serve the man of God. Even though my wife understood that everyone is called to serve his leader in some capacity, she also knew that there were others who have a special grace for serving. She didn't try to persuade me to preach or teach, but she continually encouraged me to serve the man of God.

I'm glad that I recognized this call of servant hood many years ago. It had been prophesied to me years earlier that I would be close to the man of God and released to greater measures of ministry through serving my leader.

My wife understood that by serving the man of God that our family would have to make some sacrifices. She witnessed firsthand the sacrifices made by other armourbearers and myself. My wife has had to make sacrifices too. She has had to drive herself to church, take care of the kids by herself, and give up spending time with me sometimes on holidays and anniversaries. There was one particular occasion that my wife and I planned to celebrate together. We agreed to sacrifice it so that I could travel with my pastor. My wife had no reservations because she knew it was kingdom business. It was a test to see if we were willing to sacrifice it all for the kingdom. Nevertheless, we passed the test, and as a result we received a tremendous blessing from the Lord. Time and time again my wife sacrificed because she believed in my ministry to our pastor and knew that it was not about her.

On the same token, I also understood that I needed to make sure home was taken care of first. I would stay in constant contact with my wife while I was out of town, and I would get someone to help her with the kids because both of our kids were young during this time.

Not only has my wife had to make sacrifices, but my kids have had to give up much too. Of course any child would love to have his dad with them all the time. But my kids have accepted the call on my life as well.

My wife and I believe that we are blessed today because of my decision to answer the call of serving the man of God. She has no reservations in releasing me to serve my pastor because she knows that I am doing what God has called me to do, I am receiving wisdom from the man of God, and I have access and privilege to other men and women of God that most people do not. Both of us have had the opportunity to meet some of God's finest ministry gifts. The Lord knew what He was doing. We are reminded that to whom much is given much is required. Nothing happens without purpose. All of these things have taken place because I was in my rightful position serving the man of God, and we know that God is going to continue using servant hood to catapult us to the next level.

CHAPTER LIFE APPLICATIONS

_____

_____

_____

_____

_____

_____

_____

_____

_____

_____

_____

_____

_____

_____

_____

_____

_____

CHAPTER 16
UNITY AMONG ARMOURBEARERS

Fulfill ye my joy, that ye be likeminded, having the same love, being of one accord, of one mind. Let nothing be done through strife or vainglory; but in lowliness of mind let each esteem other better than themselves. Look not every man on his own things, but every man also on the things of others.
Philippians 2:2-4

Armourbearers must have a spirit of unity among themselves. If they are going to serve the man of God they have to be on one accord with the other armourbearers. How can armourbearers protect the anointing on their leader's life if they have strife among themselves? In this chapter I would like to deal with some scriptures on unity that will bring light to this topic.

In order for the ministry of the armourbearer to be effective there has to be like-mindedness and love among the armourbearers. If one person is thinking about doing something that is not in line with the way the man of God wants to do it, it could bring shame to that house. Armourbearers must also have the same love for their leader and one another.

Let's look at some nuggets concerning unity.

- An organization that is divided will not last (Mark 3:25).

- Unity is pleasant (Psalms 133:1).

- There is strength in numbers (Ecclesiastes 4:9).

- A three-fold cord is not easily broken (Ecclesiastes 4:12).

- Double-mindedness brings about instability (James 1:8).

- The enemy loves to destroy unity (Mark 3:25).

- God rewards the agreement of His people (Matthew 18:19).

CHAPTER LIFE APPLICATIONS

_____

_____

_____

_____

_____

_____

_____

_____

_____

_____

_____

_____

_____

_____

_____

_____

ABOUT THE AUTHOR

Elder Keith Moore has served as senior armourbearer for Bishop Steven W. Banks at Living Waters Christian Fellowship in Newport News, Virginia, for over eight years. He has unabashedly and cordially heeded the clarion call to serve in this capacity. His sacrifice is undisputedly what God is requiring of each of us regardless of our function within the body of Christ.

Elder Keith's willingness to accept his calling has freed Bishop Banks from many day-to-day tasks and concerns that might otherwise hinder his ability to enter into and remain in the presence of God. His heart is forever knitted to that of Bishop Banks, and the body of Christ has been blessed and enriched because of it.

Elder Keith's subjugation has hastened the outpouring of God's blessings in his life and that of his family. His faithfulness in another man's vineyard has been rewarded with one of his own. In 2004 Elder Keith released his first book, *Revealing Christ in the Tabernacle,* which re-introduced the importance of the Tabernacle into the life of the contemporary believer. Now he is back with a newly inspired word for the body designed to encourage and empower each of us to fulfill our purpose within our local churches.

With his most recent release he is calling all of us back to the heart of God through servant hood. Servant hood does not seek out the choicest assignments but desires to embody the heart of Christ through the excellency of service it renders behind the scene. This book really reminds us that just as *every joint supplies,* if you are not doing your part the body is not complete.

Elder Keith gives thanks for his wife, Elder Connie, for releasing him to serve in this manner. Without her release his ministry would be hollow. As he reminds us in this book, a man must first provide for his own household before he takes care of another's. Elder Keith has not sacrificed his family upon the altar and left them there but he and Elder Connie respect their individual callings and submit their marriage unto the authority of God. Their children Keith Jr. and Keilah also support their dad as he ministers to others. His family's unswerving support allows him to travel, protect, and serve his leader.

This prolific teacher has been called for such a time as this and his pen points the way for a new generation. With fresh coals of fire upon his tongue, he has given voice to the anointing that rests within. He credits Pastor Chris Jordan of Unity of Faith Worship Center in Rocky Mount, North Carolina for seeing not only the Jesus within him but also the great exploits that were to come. Pastor Chris' mentorship stretched, shaped, and equipped him for the journey ahead.